D0982595

Animal Families

Written by Tom Donegan
Reading consultants: Christopher Collier and Alan Howe,
Bath Spa University, UK

First published by Parragon in 2011

Parragon
Queen Street House
4 Queen Street
Bath BA1 1HE, UK

ISBN 978-1-4454-3002-7

Printed in China

Discovery KIDS™

Animal Families

LIVE. LEARN. DISCOVER.

Bath · New York · Singapore · Hong Kong · Cologne · Delhi
Melbourne · Amsterdam · Johannesburg · Auckland · Shenzhen

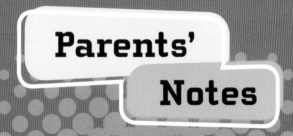

Parents' Notes

This book is part of a series of non-fiction books designed to appeal to children learning to read.

Each book has been developed with the help of educational experts.

At the end of each book is a quiz to help your child remember the information and the meanings of some of the words and sentences. There is also a glossary of difficult words relating to the subject matter in the book, and an index.

CONTENTS

ANIMAL FAMILIES

There are many types of animal families and they are all different. Bringing the next **generation** safely into the world is not easy and there are many challenges along the way. Animals overcome these challenges in many different ways.

Some animals give birth to live offspring. Others lay eggs, which **hatch** later on. Some make really good parents. Others leave their babies to look after themselves. Some animals gather in large groups, while others prefer to parent alone. Some build nests to shelter the young. Others use their own body as a mobile nursery.

This book will teach you more about how different kinds of animal families work— from the best dads to the biggest babies!

LAND
MAMMALS

Land mammals come in all shapes and size: Mothers normally give birth to their young, instead of laying eggs, and feed them milk that they produce.

Gray wolves may look fierce, but they are very caring when it comes to raising their young. The whole **pack** helps with the chores, such as bringing food back to the den.

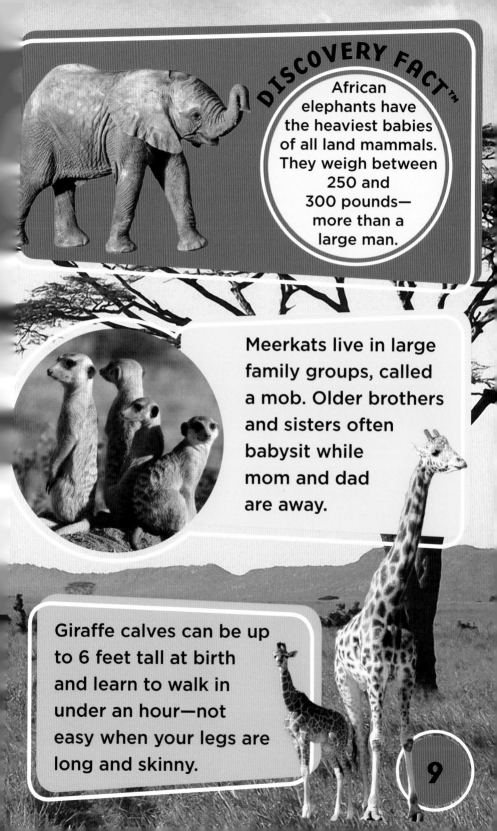

African elephants have the heaviest babies of all land mammals. They weigh between 250 and 300 pounds—more than a large man.

Meerkats live in large family groups, called a mob. Older brothers and sisters often babysit while mom and dad are away.

Giraffe calves can be up to 6 feet tall at birth and learn to walk in under an hour—not easy when your legs are long and skinny.

9

MARSUPIALS

Marsupials have a very unusual way of looking after their babies, which are called joeys. When the joey is born, it crawls into a special **pouch** on mommy's tummy. This kangaroo joey is waiting until it is strong enough to face the outside world.

After spending its first six months living inside mom's pouch, the koala joey is ready to come out into the open. However, it still spends most of its time clinging tightly onto mom!

Tasmanian devils are the largest meat-eating marsupials on the planet—around the size of a small dog. A mother can keep up to four joeys in her pouch at one time.

DISCOVERY FACT™

Virginia opossums are the only marsupials living in the wild in North America. They have the largest families of any marsupial, with the female able to carry up to thirteen joeys in her pouch!

PRIMATES

Chimpanzee moms carry their babies everywhere with them for the first five months.

They spend hours cleaning them, feeding them, and playing with them, too. Young chimps like to be tickled, just like human babies!

Gorilla babies learn to crawl at two months and walk upright at nine months.

12

Spider monkeys have strong tails. They use them to swing from tree to tree. When the babies are small, they wrap their tails around their mother to help stay on her back.

Marmosets are very small monkeys who are very caring when it comes to raising babies. The whole extended family helps out with the chores. They will carry and share food with the young, even when they are not their parents.

13

RODENTS

Baby beavers are called kits. For the first month of their lives, the kits will stay in the family lodge. A lodge is a special home made out of sticks and mud that is built in the middle of a pond.

Like many smaller rodents, baby chipmunks are born without fur, and are blind and deaf. At a week old, they start to grow fur. After a month, their eyes and ears open and they start to explore.

Flying squirrels have skin flaps between their arms and legs that they use to glide between trees. At around six weeks old, the young are ready to start practicing this unusual skill.

Porcupines are famous for their long, sharp quills, which they use for defense. A baby porcupine is born with soft quills, but they begin to harden after an hour or two.

BIRDS

Most birds build nests out of twigs and leaves, where they can keep their eggs safe and warm until they hatch.

Ducklings form a very close bond with their mother from the moment they hatch. They will follow her wherever she goes, forming a line behind her!

ying squirrel   Tasmanian devil   humpback whale

ameleon   chimpanzee   gorilla baby   marmoset

bra finch   lemon shark   ringed seal   joey

eerkats   beaver kit   rattlesnake   lodge

orcupine   ducklings   pack   shoal   alligator

adpole   python   African elephant   tail

olphin   sea otter   sea horse   nest   eggs

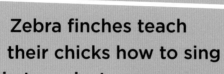

Zebra finches teach their chicks how to sing in tune, just like human babies learn to talk by listening to their parents.

DISCOVERY FACT™

The ostrich is the world's biggest bird and also lays the biggest eggs. At over 3 pounds, they weigh over 20 times as much as a chicken's egg!

REPTILES

Different kinds of snakes have very different types of families. Most snakes lay eggs, but rattlesnakes give birth to live young.

Pythons are known to be very good parents. They protect their eggs in specially made nests until they hatch.

18

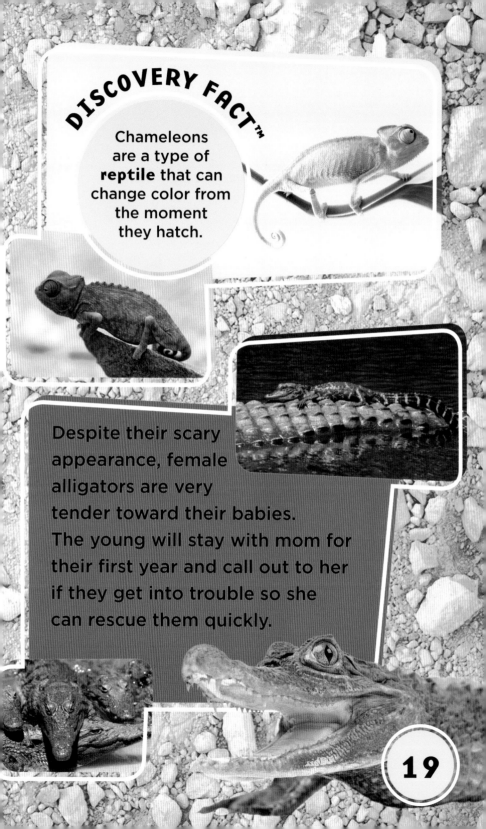

Chameleons are a type of **reptile** that can change color from the moment they hatch.

Despite their scary appearance, female alligators are very tender toward their babies. The young will stay with mom for their first year and call out to her if they get into trouble so she can rescue them quickly.

19

AMPHIBIANS

Amphibians lay eggs that usually hatch into **tadpoles** in water. The tadpoles breathe through gills, like fish. Tadpoles change into adults through a process known as **metamorphosis**.

Frog parents usually leave their tadpoles. However, the male strawberry poison dart frog will carry his baby tadpoles on his back until he finds a safe pool of water to use as a nursery.

Some kinds of toad take better care of their babies than others. After the female midwife toad has laid her eggs, the male carries them wrapped around his back legs to protect them until the tadpoles are ready to hatch.

Male Darwin's frogs help keep their young away from predators by putting them inside the large vocal pouch in their throat!

21

SEA

MAMMALS

Dolphin families are known as pods. Family life is very important to dolphins, who work together to hunt fish and care for the young.

Ringed seals live in the Arctic, where the sea freezes for much of the year. They dig caves in the ice, which shelter their pups from the cold.

Baby blue whales drink 100 gallons of milk and gain 200 pounds in weight in a day!

Every year, humpback whales migrate thousands of miles across the oceans. If a humpback calf gets tired during the journey, its mother will nudge it along with her nose and keep it near the surface so it can breathe.

Sea otters can sleep while floating on the water's surface. Family members hold hands so they do not drift away while taking a nap.

FISH

Almost all fish lay eggs, which then hatch into tiny **fry**. Many fry, such as baby salmon, start life with a yolk sac still attached to their underside, which they eat

Mouthbreeders are a group of fish that use their large mouths to keep their eggs warm. They will often carry the fry in their mouths, too

Many kinds of fish swim together in large groups called shoals. These extended families provide protection, especially for the younger fish, because predators become confused by the huge numbers all moving quickly together.

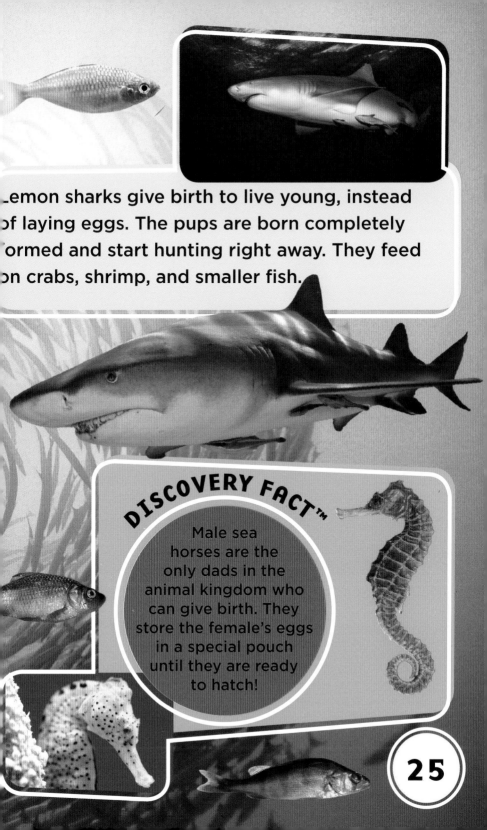

Lemon sharks give birth to live young, instead of laying eggs. The pups are born completely formed and start hunting right away. They feed on crabs, shrimp, and smaller fish.

DISCOVERY FACT™

Male sea horses are the only dads in the animal kingdom who can give birth. They store the female's eggs in a special pouch until they are ready to hatch!

QUIZ

Now try this quiz!
All the answers can be found in this book.

1. How tall can giraffe calves be at birth?

a) 4 feet
b) 5 feet
c) 6 feet

2. How long do chimpanzee moms carry their babies around for after birth?

a) Five months
b) Six months
c) Seven months

3. What are baby beavers called?

a) Calves
b) Kits
c) Joeys

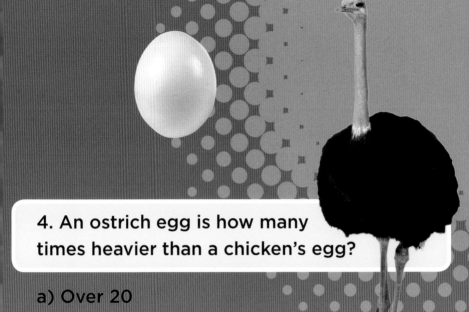

4. An ostrich egg is how many times heavier than a chicken's egg?

a) Over 20
b) Over 25
c) Over 30

5. Which baby animal drinks 100 gallons of milk and gains 200 pounds in weight in a day?

a) Humpback calf
b) Baby blue whale
c) Lemon shark pup

6. What is a large group of fish swimming together called?

a) Fry
b) Pouch
c) Shoal

GLOSSARY

Amphibians   Animals with cold blood that start life in water as tadpoles when they're born, before changing into adults and coming on to dry land.

Fry   Young fish that have just hatched from their eggs.

Generation   A set of members of a family born from the same parents. You are the next generation from your parents.

Hatch   When a baby emerges from its egg.

Marsupials   Mammals that carry their babies in a special pouch after they have been born.

28

Metamorphosis   The process of when tadpoles of amphibians change into adults, by growing arms and legs and usually losing their tails.

Pack   A group of wild animals that live and hunt together.

Pouch   A pocket on a marsupial mother's tummy where the young are carried after birth.

Reptiles   Cold-blooded animals with dry, scaly skin that keep warm by basking in the sun.

Rodents   Mammals with strong front teeth that never stop growing, so that they have to constantly wear them down to keep them the correct length.

Tadpoles   The young of amphibians. They hatch in water and have tails and gills.

INDEX

ACKNOWLEDGMENTS

All images are from istockphoto

32